WAVELAND

WAVELAND

ÖSEL JESSICA PLANTE

www.blacklawrence.com

Executive Editor: Diane Goettel
Cover Design: Zoe Norvel
Cover Art: "Latourel Falls" by Alexander Iversen-Cress
Book Design: Amy Freels

Published 2021 by Black Lawrence Press.
Printed in the United States.

for my Mother
for my Father

CONTENTS

Two: Crow & Bone

One: The Navy Wife

"You will hear thunder and
remember me and think:
she wanted storms."

~Anna Akhmatova~

Assembling the Navy Wife

Fragile, hollow—I make a new woman
from these animal bones, a ghost that will disregard
roof and walls. Cardinals come to collect
her marginalia, drift in and out
of her ribs. If these birds had names, she would
call them *Daughter I Do Not Have*, *Mother
of Pearl*, *Herring Bone*. They button their past
tense into her body as they swoop in cursive.
She is not held together by muscle
or tendon, but brittle memory,
the sinew and gut used to sew flesh
to animal hide; my fingers grow stiff
around my needle. This is not a contract,
these stitches, yet here I am trapping myself
inside her. She'll never know
that I talk to a piece of red linen
as if it is her soul. Leave your dead by
the roadside, leave your wells covered, there are
so many ways to die yet every day
she'll live as if by habit. Breathe in, breathe out.
But, it's I who might blow out the lights, drop
her hand, extinguish an entire town
with the waves gathered beneath her gown.

Pistol of Bones

I live in a green house on First Street
like a figment passing through rooms,

almost less than plaster and lathe, horse
-hair smoothed into walls, pine trees felled

a hundred years before I drank the sun
and rain, rooted deep in silence and sleep

married to a man who flooded our
bedroom each night, never sat at the table

to eat, nor took his pleasure in me. Listen
to the way *oh* is the surprise we know

with our mouths—my moon, my cottage,
my storms that blew acorns onto the tin

roof. I measure and sew my days
together—floral and nothing I would

buy again or hang myself in a new life,
the one without a man, the one where I

understand the marrow of words tastes
nothing like the marrow of bones.

The Navy Wife Talks in Her Sleep

You are a deer, my Dear, and not quite
here, so I am alone and braid this green season
into our empty house which in me is like a singed
piece of silver thread being stitched through my center
as all new homes are, and unfamiliar. Marriage is
not salvation; it is waking with horses in a field,
an apple resting in dirt, a deer with its belly
slashed open, iron leaves of blood. My husband does not
draw the knots out of my tongue. Somewhere the redbud
trees are blooming the way bodies bloom beneath the earth,
full of what they've left undone, and *oh*, tell me I'm
not the only one who fears having her center plundered
and known. I set out a bowl of red plums and study
their skins from the other side of the room until my skin too
is drenched. I'm red as a bowl full of cardinals clustered
together before they break away. I've watched a female
flit in and out of the chain link fence and see the male
follow her to gulp down her dusk. Isn't he bright, the way
he takes her everything? These are the mornings of black
snakes looking for warmth on rocks, and the blood smell
thick and heady drawing mosquitoes, the moan of the trees
protesting the wind, and the harmless distance of the stars' light
we cannot see by day. This is not to say one of us is the deer
and the other is night, or earth, or the green of a summer
evening, but that we are the dark with antlers by the roadside
and spring grass grown high, the cricket chirp and gravel
dirt crunch-scuffed beneath boots, the headlight beams
into a slice of country and a fence, yes, the way fences
pretend to hold back fields which can never be held.

The Navy Wife's Alphabet

Night grows beneath the skin of my wrists
and I'm tilted on my axis, looking out the window

at a black cat climbing through the branches
of a cottonwood tree. This world

with no edges, and another midnight I've promised
to someone dear and lost, the slow drag

down to nothing that makes me
believe in the truth of the church

sign which reads: *Are you a figment*
of someone else's imagination? Like trying

to train horses to gallop on leashes.
Love, I am alone with an entire alphabet

carved into the gnarled bark of trees, four initials
at a time and all those signs—plus, plus, plus.

She Contemplates Autumn

It was the year we'd replanted
the old garden—the rhubarb still sturdy
and bitter, the compost pile full of oyster shells.

Leaning out our window at night I'd memorize
each feral sound, the animals that would keep me,
how the stars represented love as a series

of distances. I knew that an inexact heart could
build its own wilderness. Whether or not I wanted,
black snakes lived near the tuberoses, & the blueberry

shrubs grew laden with tart indigo suns. I'd lie
awake at night beside him feeling nothing
but their blue skins, and instead of smoothing

them, in the morning, I'd begin by tossing
the comforter over the rumpled sheets. Already
I had learned how to live on what I alone could

gather. What I imagined marriage gave me was
no more than the maple flaming at the end of our
driveway, which would someday soften into to ash.

Instructions on Becoming a French Prostitute

Move to Paris. Practice rolling your tongue past words
like *Les Fleurs du Mal*, your lips as they grip every *vous*.
Do this while brushing your hair in the nude, never naked,
always nude. Acquaint yourself with lingerie, the exquisite
hand-tatted lace, rough-edged where the silk threads end
between your legs. Your legs, your bangs soft trimmed
straight, eyelashes coated with thick charcoal dust. By now
you've studied the soft lamb-skin wallets in hotel bars,
the blends of silk and wool suits, scarlet linings. Change
your name to Scarlet, your number on speed dial, elevators
and keycard access, your white leather bag filled with
tight jeans, dark glasses (for after). His silver hair recedes,
and a firm careless hand moves through you. Diamond
-mouthed you take him, leaving nothing of yourself.

She & Wolf

Outside my house there are men heating up
the newly paved road with a blow torch. Their fire

sounds like an airplane engine. In orange
and yellow vests they make me think of what needs

protection, not the fruit of the fig tree from
wasps which will burrow deep inside, not the tadpoles

birthed into the brackish shallows that will
nibble an outstretched palm, but the piece of me still

circling into my husband's ear, his mouth,
measuring herself against his bones as I sit aching

at my desk, bent and white as a swan, hollow
as honeysuckle wrists. The wind blowing outside ruffles

the men's hair. They parade back and forth
to their truck like peacocks, their words dissolve before

I can hear. My husband's words have found
the shady edges like snow in early spring, they glint

from the sunless rims like amber holds a frozen
sun. Look and there's the curve of a beetle's wing, a tiny

continent of stillness, dust. Any warmth now
and my scars flare. The life below the one that shows,

wriggling to come, to know itself black as tar
and indistinguishable after the men are done. I get up,

head for the kitchen to dive into lunch. The coral
mouth of a torch goes out, there are small fires sutured

to me tight as a blush. I wish for a dozen birds,
for sunlight to strike my throat ruby, bare—a woman,

a bell, a magnolia bloom, the same uninvited
wolf sitting in my dining room chair.

When the Mississippi Speaks with its Wet, Pretty Mouth

A string of vowels comes out, silty tongue
curling under and around the dark outside

the Highlife Bar that backs up to this brackish
curl of coast. You need a passport to come

this far South, where men with flashlights
wade knee-deep with spears, flick them into

dark so their small beacons appear to nod
like drunken heads. I watch for silhouettes,

men gigging for flounder that lie flat in mud
they've burrowed under with one eye facing

up to stars. Out beyond the naked bay, Pass
Christian in the grip of old growth pines once

felled for floors now in turn-of-century homes
full of double-hung windows the Preservation

Society adores. I'm with my husband, who's
ordered another Michelob Ultra as I finger

a fried pickle out of the plastic basket lined
with waxed paper now translucent with

grease. He asks if I want another, if I want
to dance upstairs then stares at the lights

of a distant gulf shrimp boat where the hearts
of a few men bob, they're trawling for someone

else's dinner, throwing back rusted cans and gar
fish, while upstairs the bartender calls me

"Little Lady" and I am still when my husband grabs
and flings the ring toss game on its string, I am

remembering the antique fan I'd brought from
Boston which he carried to the attic because it

was too rustic, the bicycle I rode through Nova
Scotia with my father he put out with the trash

when I went home to visit my mother. Just a ring
on a dingy string, we watch its elliptical flight how

it seeks the clink of collision. I think about how
my name is no longer my name and how I am full

of the same old dumb luck that sent me up
the aisle at twenty-eight, though he did not know

how I was afraid to be alone. Another quarter
dropped into the juke box slot, the air along

the Gulf is stagnant, hot. My hair pinned up
off my nape and he's not touched me in several

nights, not a wrist or hip but I am all right
with how we shift in bed after the lights go out,

listen as a distant train approaches the trestle
over the bay & soon we'll walk out to our car,

I'll take the keys but only after we've chugged
another each, listen as records shift and drop,

Etta James begins to sing, her voice moving east
then south like a knife through me, like I'm some

small town with the word pearl in it, then Slidell,
over denim-colored Lake Pontchartrain, its palms

open, how it rises each time it rains, and there,
once, how a woman flashed a gun at me on

I-10 after I'd merged, speeding into her lane.

Slow Parting

I lie down in the dry grass before each winter
and rise to meet the rain. Together we begin

to skirt the cedar trees, drive the red-winged
blackbirds out of the cattails where they've crazed

in pairs and threes all fall. Long ago I'd heard
the sycamores marring their own bark,

again. From the inside they tore themselves
into gray childish shapes, as if in need of the kind

of touch that follows a scar. As the rivulets
of evening grew colder between us you kept

forgetting to shut the doors. I'd watch you retreat
to your office, or go out for a run past the houses—

identical on that flat square of earth we called home.
I'd wash dishes, then listen to you take a shower.

Some days I'd ask you to pick me up and carry me
in buckets and bowlfuls to the bedroom. At least

a husband should be able to drown inside his wife.
I was a pond swelled past its meager banks.

Her Notes on Keeping Silent

When one part of me recedes over a hill, another part
is watching my back, as though I'm also the horse

in the field below that recognizes me as the woman who
walks each morning to the edge of what she must believe

in. We're two figures in a painting that's never been
painted. It's October with an ovation of leaves and pastures

so numerous the sky must be jealous. I've always liked
this turning and falling, a time for everything to come

undone, though I'm no closer, and the silence I carry
has grown heavier than the one I was born with. This place

is just the same, an old story passed around a fire,
or with fire, which I've been told is the only language

the heart speaks in. We forget we're not these pieces,
that which is cold, the blue that's held us—or like dock

or mint, the first bitter taste that filled us. We are salt
strung thick on its thread, the seeing and the unsaid.

Poem with a Mouse & a Line by Larry Levis

Our bedroom was windowless, a place where light
went to die, the backyard wild with vine-buckled

chain link, and somewhere behind the refrigerator,
or in the dank beneath the sink, a mouse made

itself familiar with things we did not wish to see;
as we ate dinner, or watched TV it left droppings

between spoons and knives, would bite the corners
off bags of brown sugar and Basmati rice. We were

sleeping together again, but this time the central air
had gone, the mattress pulled onto the living room

floor beneath where a single window unit chugged.
We'd closed all the doors. It was early July. I was

still in the habit of being in love. The rain drummed
the sides of our duplex as you quoted your gospel,

that *a body wishes to be held, & held, & what can
you do about that?* I knew how to break a heart,

my own, already alone sitting on that mattress
like an island of cling, we clung to each other a little

longer than we should, to what we had left
—the mouse scurrying, all night, all along the edge.

The Navy Husband Digs a Pool

For days he drove a bright yellow Bobcat
to move earth from the center of our yard,

he piled dirt along the back fence, exhausted
and measured our plot beneath the hot sun,

wresting all that had lain undisturbed, patchy
grass where oleander had stood, a place

to put the dog, a yard smaller than a postage
stamp on a zoning map folded into a drawer.

Day or night, what I couldn't abide he dragged
around for all to see until what began as

a depression one day had corners and walls
of dirt after a crew of men shaped the pit

he'd dug. They secured steel rods into the earth,
a concrete truck split our driveway in two.

The slurry would set in three days he said, & as it
cures will emit a chemical heat. At night I'd step

outside to water it with the hose. Though it had no
drain, nor lights, for years he'd fill & swim until

one evening I stripped and waded in. The air was
warm, the house had sold, he lived in another

town; I took my turn swimming laps & floating
on my back, in the center of what he'd exhumed.

Naked in Cowboy Boots with Lasso, I Challenge God

You do not ask but enter our neighborhoods, circle our cul-de-sacs,
blare the silence into our yards and synapses, into my sink
of unwashed dishes while the cats cower in the bed sheets. I have

begged and received one divorce, two pregnancies which ended
with the black dot and dirty rag of surgery, the memory of longing
sunk by grief, a cold cactus on a desert night and somewhere out

there my ex-husband wandering. But now my heart is elastic as a lasso
I've reeled in to knock the dust from my boots. A full cast of stars
clicking in the night sky. I let my arm fly again and pull them in

for a kiss, forgiveness, to catch what was never mine. I'm learning
to bend and give until I hold drops of dew on each needle for lizards
to tongue—my lost sons. Because everything deserves relief,

because I've grown strong this way, letting out a little more rope
each night growing more and more still as if to burst from all
I accommodate inside these spurs and bones, inside the curve

my arm makes as I wave goodbye with my rope dragging
more and more darkness out of a sky that feasts on God's one
good eye, the closed one, the one he uses to measure us by.

The Navy Wife's Plan for Her Wedding Dress

It's time to get rid of it, stained now and the stitching
in the armpits torn from dancing, a dribble of gravy

on the bodice set into the satin. Silent and full of air
where my body once stood beside him, that day in church,

the priest who barely knew us. Vintage, 1930s, the kind
of dress with a story to tell. At the reception

my aunts exclaimed over the fabric—opalescent,
golden-hued, a patina rich and lit from within. Maybe

that's why I'd bought it months before we'd even met.
I'd wanted another dream to tape shut in a box and stick

in a closet. My mother paid to have scraps cut
from the hem and waist; two women turned about

me with pins between their lips, my body draped
in too much white. I will burn it at the stake; suspend it

on a limb of the oak tree in my backyard. Light a fire
—then watch as the hem catches in a ring of rose-gold

flame, burning away the hips and bust, pintucks
and covered buttons, everything he's ever touched.

Disassembling the Navy Wife

After he was not there it seemed terrible
to have ever loved him. It was June,

the dead pine needles still on the ground. Piece by piece
I left myself. In this room my hair and my right

eye, in this a femur bone. In his old office
I kept my father's hands. In the attic, the daughter

we'd never had. One day I forgot the difference
between my memory and what was

missing. I started thinking about myself all the time,
found a man who lived inside my skull,

found him and decided to bury him outside the empty house
where the trees don't move. After twenty years

I cut the trees down and built a boat, slipped out
beyond the oars to whisper to the water the story

where God has a son but no daughter. He cannot
speak. Some men don't know they're unhappy.

I take a folding chair and sit outside, measure
the length of the day against what I need—sky

like a blue shirt waving in the branches, cardinal

like a red scar veining through the leaves, my body
which pulls the blade from everything.

We Forget Our Always

I've seen a hummingbird the past two days
stitching through my waking hours,

the wild edge, the void. I wait for the geraniums
to uproot their blaze-red heads and transplant

me to another dimension. Their roots dangle
into the same dark abyss from which a man

emerges pushing his blue bicycle.
A train whistle bleats its horned head

then passes into the stillness that's everywhere
the sum zero of existence. Inside me

time's just like yesterday. No need to leave
the doors unlocked, or the porch

lights on. We said our I love yous but gave less
than the fronds of a fern. We dug holes

deep as the world, then poured into each other
our nevers, not enoughs, our always. We cancelled

forever with our promises, just to carry on.

Unfuckable Poem

Misery finds its way into the populace,
sits on a riverbank, pisses in the water
supply, reaches up a young girl's shirt
fondles her breasts so that the horse
in her ribs bucks and her mouth goes
dry. The universe is like a wide eye inside
her eye, inside a city that never blinks.
Truck stop, fuck you, and the blistered
asphalt and whatever guy who's waiting
in his office on this Friday afternoon at 4:30
listening to the bricks tighten in their mortar.
How 'bout we go out and dig worms
for date night, how 'bout we throw out
the Ikea directions. All day I've been drinking
like I live inside a Sharon Van Etten song,
some part of my brain bleeding, another part
soaking the stain in OxiClean. You kept trying
to correct my imperfections but they
kept changing. Here, run your fingers over
this bicycle chain while it's slipping my greased
gears. Yesterday I thought of the way
he used to love me, like I was a moving target
and he had no aim or balance. Now I want him
to care again so I can tell him to stop hovering.
Some days, in his absence, I'd even accuse air
and music of breaking and entering. Some days
misery sounds like Missouri, and we all
live there, every last one.

After Joining OkCupid

I'd like to confess that dating four men at once
is kind of awesome, the way the heart knows how
to expand and break off into knowledgeable pieces
occurs quite naturally, and because one of the men

happens to be a micro-economist who studies
game theory, I've begun to consider the nature
of scarcity, how I am like a commodity where desire
is the only available currency and since another

is a translator I'll ask, *how do I say the heart is a vagrant*
in Polish, and he might reply, in the spirit of love
and conversion, that I must loiter long enough
in a foreign territory to understand the principles

at play. The other two, a musician and a biologist,
have led me to expect that by the end of the month
I'll have found that the best way for the body to hold
its own concert is by singeing all my organs simultaneously

through the fire of orgasm; however, if this seems
like too much information, try disconnecting from your
deepest sense of longing long enough to take in the world
at its pleasurable best. After all, our planet is something

like a cruise ship with its mid-west buffets of grain
and its lit-up cities that bi-coastally drift on the plate
of our hemisphere. You've seen those NASA
satellite photos of earth from space, how we're

congealed in darkness like a terabyte of light bulbs tossed in the air. It can make you want to catch your breath, the beauty of the cosmos, or just some new stranger standing in front of you in his underpants.

Like a Fish Needs a Bicycle

There's something crooked about his mouth,
and though he's obviously going to go bald
someday soon, his eyebrows are like kind, squat
temples above his eyes, one pupil dilated
slightly more than the other. This is what it's like
to be single—to stare at a picture of a man online
and wonder, what does he smell like? What
would it feel like to wake up beside him after
two years of living together? I want
to believe that all relationships are mistakes
waiting to happen, have that built-in obsolescence
and are the reason why I finally like that saying
about the woman, a fish, and a bicycle. I like imagining
a cartoon fish upright underwater with its fins
spinning in loose circles the same way we pedal
our feet in the air during yoga to warm up
our thighs. Love's made a fool of me once
too often. It's like standing over a car engine—
I don't know the rules for recalibrating
or even how to change the oil. It's just that
every man looks like laundry and concession, even
the doctor with great abs my sister tells me she's seen
at the soccer field with his son. Does he wake
in the morning and cook his kid oatmeal? Where is
his ex-wife now and has she felt it, how love is
at first a greening, how even the bright trees
shuddering their shadows across our faces seem
a delicious sensation. I wonder that we're able to hold

in abeyance the blade that will come to cut away all
that softness and leave in its place the ribs of something
enormous like the hull of a shipwreck, love having split
a way for something new, the bones of the world exposed.

The Goddess of Confusion

What did it mean when the bird shit in my iced tea
as we circled the pond on a blind date is not a question
I ever thought I'd ask myself, though I've been looking

for meaning in the strangest places lately, like ankle injuries
that make it harder to escape ideas of fragility or how seeing
a fox in my neighbor's yard could be auspicious, since I

believe in spirit animals, the power of lunar eclipses, and rose
quartz crystals. Why not, since we don't know the inner lives
of stone or what it feels like to be a pink rag of cloud swabbed

across the sky? *Let the inanimate animate our lives* says my friend,
the Goddess of Confusion, who recently asked me to no longer call
her the Goddess of Confusion because she's been settled now

for three weeks on the same guy. Amazing how love can do that,
pull us into orbit when we've been wobbling on an axis
of cat adoption, tarot cards, and Tennessee. But I'm alone now

on a trail at Maclay Gardens thinking about forgiveness and how
the heart goes to hell when it's not given, or how it can feel
like several wheelbarrows left out in the rain, and because

I can't solve my grievances or OxiClean my history back
to tabula rasa. Instead, out here, I want to high five the older
woman for walking her two mutts with such gusto, the man

who huffs up on his bicycle and pants at the view—a lake full
of lily pads and alligators which I can say looks almost beautiful.
What I do is read the trail map which shows I'm on a red line

that wraps around water, find a dropped cardinal feather to stick
in my car's dash, study an autumn full of red and orange leaves,
their falling ovation. I try to obey a carved wooden plaque that states

Sensitive area, please keep on trail, while my mind insists that I
wander, try to figure out how this body first became one part rain
two parts fire, elements through which we exit and enter.

Go to the Edge of Giving Then Break Yourself

This is the advice I get from the universe, or rather
from an astrologer who's giving his report by a duck
    pond in New Zealand; he talks about Mars and Jupiter,
the energy of all exotic creatures, of which the duck
    is not one. Distracted, I glaze the surface of his words
like the duck nuzzling its feathers, or some algae, or is
    it his partner's reflection? One duck plus one duck
equals a pastime to throw bread at, a puzzle of innocence,
    reason not to say, "majestic creatures." *The new moon,*
he says, *enters Sagittarius.* My new partner thinks I can never
    be serious, but I want to get below, or be brought low by
him, to give until I'm like a holiday party after the candles
    have sputtered out, after the guests have left and the wine
has set in the carpet. I'll waddle to him on hands & knees
    so he can see what he's done, plumping my feathers,
tipping over for him, pouring out until he can no longer
    doubt his love. So, I watch astrology reports about how
the heavens move, a science of looking for clues & last
    night he saw me taste him in the lemon rinds I bit, taking
them off the water glass rim, *for bioflavonoids*, I said.
    I need these distractions, these planets of laughter, giving
all I have to everyone I paddle past because I can't wrap
    him in all my affection. I make my way towards him
afraid to knock stars out of their constellations. Holding
    my breath, I flicker through a bruise-like emptiness.

Peaches

The problem with words now is that they don't
break open the way I broke open,

they can't hold or move or bend unless
I am standing knee deep in the ocean and I am

almost never standing in the ocean,
not that way, not anymore. I would buy

two Moscow mules and walk towards the waves,
pour one into the blue mouth

that used to know me. I'd blink inside its eye
and now, nothing knows me. No one

knows. Once, I was raped and that is what I thought
life was, the exhaustion of giving yourself

to every mud-slicked face that can say your name.
Everyone I meet says my name, so who

can I blame for the woman inside me
who calls herself an animal, angel, or bruise

of yesterday? Look, life doesn't go away
just because you feel you're less than an embryo.

I find peaches in my hands all the time
so I eat them. Just like anyone else.

Waveland Mississippi, an Elegy

Treaded and unlaced by the cattails the dun-
colored sneaker lies forgotten and all things

weighing the same in my mind it swims away
like our home in Mississippi which once

unfettered from slab and sky became part of
the storm surge, because "wind-blown water"

is not the same as "hurricane" we'd learn when
our Allstate claim was denied. Before the storm

we used to hang with Masey, the neighbor's
gardener, and because I was shy and young I'd

take the mondo grass she'd give me to plant
in the too deep gully in our front yard. *They're*

thirsty, she'd say, the bucket of her voice
dropping its water on me but I never planted

anything she gave. Mississippi's always had
something live in its mouth, but after Katrina

I waved to Masey only once by the wreckage
of the carriage house, then went on wondering

about the stray cat I'd fed as our neighbor's car
sat slant across our yard. To think they'd been

angry when our house was built—the metal
roof, the pergola too close to the street, now our

bathtub was in the drive. I reached beneath a fallen
wall and found a loose doorknob. Ten years later

it lies in a basket of magazines, the old number 'I'
from our mailbox on the toilet tank. My roommates

don't ask what for. I don't think about my ex-husband
or miss his Navy uniforms or pick-up truck, but from

time to time I revisit the image of that mahogany
front door stained the color of mud. Six panes

of glass, I didn't care what the neighbors could see
when they drove by, couldn't be bothered, not when

the peepers grew so loud at night and the pines
cracked like knuckles in the wind, worry making me

call for the dog to come in from the yard. I'd turn
off all the lights in the house and stand, waiting

for the rain, the windows open an inch, knowing
I was alone, my bare feet on the cold hard floor.

Two: Crow & Bone

"There is this edge where shadows
and bones of some of us walk
backwards."

~Joy Harjo~

Eleven

I ride my bicycle through a country of black crows
—they cover the earth with their lurching hops
and lazy take offs. My childhood is closing like a fist
around my hair, brown vine rooted in my skull, the womb
of my brain, that will birth the real me. First time I was born
I was pulled back to the world by a goddess of rain
who tacked the thirst of a field of high grass in September
to my back. I rubbed my back on the black walnut tree
in the center of creation until my mind flickered
like a lamp. Because this was my first life it was
there to be wasted. Years of washing my hair
thinking it was someone else's, that I needed a man,
that my days were stopped like crows along the highway
waiting to shop the carcass at their leisure after the engine
of travel had ceased, to be alone with that picture
of death, and to eat it in peace, an entire battalion
of mouths that stoops to pick what's theirs out
from loosening gravel. When I was a child I knew
none of this. I thwarted. I hid. I disguised myself from grief
until one day I began to fill with rain. To my ankles,
to my knees, when my heart was drenched a shudder
bloomed towards my brain. I grew black feathers
and wings, found the highest point within myself
and jumped. A thousand birds, a murmuration makes
its own music. It sounds like humming. I am
humming. I am plummeting. I am sails of rain.

Blue Eyed Crow

I pray that the crows will return to my yard

so I can watch them pluck off their plumes
like soft black knives, alive the way words

are alive inside the earth of our bones. Did you know

that the tongue is never empty? That it has a memory
all its own? If you were to flay mine you'd find

the letters of your name next to the ones

for God; they make an impression, a shadow that travels
backwards inside my throat along that pink hollow as if

I am a cave of honey. Come, listen to me speak. Let my mouth

move against your emptiness until you utter back to me
the sounds I most want to hear. Once spoken, a word

is fragile as music and holds no more. Today the crows

have changed my name so you'll no longer recognize me
on your tongue. You who were barely inside

me, I'd take your right eye, blue, and place it

next to its mate, arrange them like pebbles
in this dish on my desk. I know you think about

me. You've sent these crows to my yard to spy,

to arrow their wedged and dark heads down to the earth
as if they are pointing to where I've been.

It's Not an Apocalypse if the Horses are Mortal

or if they arrive several nights in a row. It will only begin when
    I am ready to walk out of my body, its slow trailer of dark

        hitched to my every move, night pushing me around,
            trying to get rid of me. Feed your darkness, it says,

know your hunger, fingering my mind, touching the shelves
    like a butcher, darkness diced, cut into even slices. I began

        to surround myself with things that were not my own,
            to enter other people's lives, study

their objects, imagine who they loved
    and why. It was a slow stroke I'd make over the skin

of their existence, the way I'd always imagined God did
to me when I was sleeping, the way I begged him to

be near me. Several times I nested my desire
for God inside the men I'd sleep with, but, like him,

I'd forget their faces, remembering only a blot of ink,
a swirl of hair. My habit was to take something

of theirs to hold onto. For one, the shape of his loneliness,
for another, a lighter, blue plastic, flicked by a thumb

that had been in my mouth only moments before. I was
trying to forget who I'd been, sitting with

my thighs crossed, switching on the light until I could
bite it in two. I imagined the sun was as real as

an empty bed, a shovel. Then I knew all
the right steps to take. First, remove the thumb

from your mouth. First, ask where else the bodies
are hidden. First, make a fist of your hand

          and strike wildly. First, bring it into a field,
    lay it down, shove a clean rag in its mouth, douse it

    in gasoline, crouch over it in the dry grass
flicking the flame of a bic, arousing it over and over.

    See its eyes reflect the heat, the warmth,
        then watch how fire can kick, watch it buck.

The Difference Between a Raven & a Crow

One is for sorrow, two for mirth, three's a wedding, four's a birth.
I see one crow flying over the car as my brother drives
us along the California coast;
we stop in Occidental, the roads switching through redwoods,
now past niche vineyards with names like Poplar Suite
No. 5 and across the Russian River, then the ocean
pealing dome-split-blued and horizon-tucked
like a mantra in the mouth. We park at Goat's Head and walk down
to the waves sucking sand down to grit, past tourists
in windbreakers, a girl wearing a tutu
over leggings, her hair curled around a wrist
of wind. I stuff my pockets with seashells, pools of whorl,
remembrances I do not need. We don't stay long
enough, maybe that's how I knew it would be so I took
all those shells. Later, I'd wash them in the guest bathroom sink
and set them, dried, on the white bedspread.
My brother had told me, as the Pacific curved its water
on our right, my palm on the leather armrest, the difference
between a crow and a raven is their size,
but also in the color and shape of their beaks,
a raven's is strong like stone and sharp enough to tear
fur from meat. But both wear their feathers black and mirrored,
I think, and when walking across snow look like men
who have lost their briefcases
or like punctuation marks wandering on a blank white page
lost between words-no-worlds, just lost, pocket squares
of blood in their hearts, tender hearts, and when
they sleep do they shut only one black eye? Five is for heaven,
six for hell, the tale ends with seven, but I think
six is enough. Let them dream with one eye open.

Self Portrait as a Delicate Fly

I ran the side of my face against the coral-hued flower
I stole from the neighbor's yard, my half-empty glass
of white wine left on the corner of their porch beneath
the Scorpio full moon. I think of the lover I left behind
in Florida, the one who has a girlfriend, the one who
walked me backwards into his bedroom to pretend at
love for a while. I wonder, Dear Dead White Dude Poets,
what advice you'd give on nights like these, the heart
a hungry animal, the usual tools laid out on the lawn,
a corpse or two shaken free from the past, dancing naked,
spectral-thin—perhaps it's just the wind. I've forced every
man I've ever loved to make me cry. I don't know why.
Yesterday I bought a black lace dress and a pair of panties
by the brand Psycho Bunny. I guess it's almost funny.

The Ant & the Our Father

I am going to Heaven must be what the ant thought as I
sucked him up in the vacuum cleaner while maneuvering
a chair from beneath the dining table at my sister's
house. Imagine the powerful upsweep of a giant's
inhalation, the lifting from linoleum of eight minuscule feet,
and the unearthly shushing—louder than a jet engine
to the one whose exoskeleton must have vibrated
with something like joy careening on the end of a leash,
like taking seventeen dogs for a walk until he finally lost
his grip and didn't care. Should I care? Should I care
about this ant, no, three or five ants I've sucked into this dirt
and dog hair Heaven? Because I once converted Buddhist?
Because I've always felt guilty even while vacuuming
another person's floors? Because Catholicism knew
how to immobilize me with its iconography, its blue
shrouded Marys, cloud-like lambs, and saints with palms
spread wide their gazes upturned since every saint needs
to keep working at the hem of their Lord's forgiveness, even
the cows in the manger looking around with perpetual
questions in their mooning eyes as if some nun might begin
to scold them and to this day (though there is no one
left to scold me) I whisper the Our Father when I'm belted
into coach, using the softest hushed and rushed syllables
as the captain hits his accelerators, and when we land again
I pull that prayer out from beneath mounds of in-flight
magazines, rustle through thoughts and words at the floor
of my mind as if a prayer is a dress I wore last Friday night
and consider wearing again—but for the lisp of a wine stain,
but for the who art of memory of last weekend's drunk

still clinging to the poly-blend fibers. Who art? Who art
in Heaven, who art with the ant, who art the maker
of the air I breathe, and the squirrel I saw this morning
stealing a strawberry, unripe, from my sister's garden,
the squirrel who knows not of guilt but in whom the Lord
dwelleth, and Lucy, the black lab whose fur clots the vacuum's
cylinder and whose wet, urgent nose sniffs at Otto, the kitten
I've brought with me from home who knoweth not
of the dog's bite and who I protect like my own tuxedoed
child born in some alley in Tallahassee, who scares at the first
sign of the vacuum, who knows Heaven is in my apartment,
its windows, its bed left unmade as I am unmade in the sight
of the Lord who dwells in the ant who now dwells inside
this vacuum, I mean Heaven, I mean this floor is clean.

Lying on a Bench in Dorothy B Oven Park I'm Mistaken for a Homeless Woman

I'm not homeless, I'm a poet, I say to the groundskeeper
who interrupts as I stare at the sky's blank arousal
thinking about love. *Is there something you need?*

the groundskeeper asks. But nothing, not even
the squirrel with her acorn has more than I do, not even
the spade in his hand has less. If, to a man

with a hammer all things look like a nail, what about
the man with a spade—do I look like the soft, mute language
of soil waiting for something where nothing is?

It's like that when I'm with you, like trying to find
the right amount of nakedness my first time
at a nudist beach, to calculate the space between

my mouth and the Pleiades. No way to fill your plate
with fire, or a minnow hiding in its silver scales
of wish, if language were an element, sturdy

enough to taste, then my body is the little hump-backed
bridge rising above this pebbled stream. I'm homeless
in the heart of this world & *yes, yes, I need everything.*

Gospel According to the Second Person

I don't want to be anywhere he's been
after the relationship ends and it's such a small town
I think, *Did he stand at this café counter*

and order the cold brew earlier today? Because
I know how he takes it and can't stop thinking
about how he took it from me; so that later when

I'm walking through woods down trails I showed
him, picking up bits of trash and stuffing them
into a Dairy Queen styrofoam cup someone's

abandoned, it's a little ironic that I also want
to burn it all down to scrub his memory from
the planet. I know that's crazy, so to get

him off my mind I fly to Costa Rica, enter
a commune to sit in silence with hippies from Israel
and Canada eating a diet of coconut and papaya

and then find myself one night fingering seashells
on a beach in Colón Panama while an Ecuadorian
shaman holds out his brew of roots, leaves,

and shoots while the moon tosses her preserver
of light over me and the ocean, speaking in a language
I now understand is one hundred percent emotion.

Tiny bird, precious girl, the brew breathes and for
a while I believe, but then, in all this knuckling under
I can't help but remember his knuckles, the backs

of his hands that reminded me so much of my
mother's, her gold rings sliding her fingers, coming to rest
against the first knot of bone, like they were looking

for a permanent home. *Take me everywhere with
you,* I'd asked him, and so he stepped me to the edge,
watched me leap, then turned, went home, made

himself a sandwich, and wrote a song about a girl
he used to love, whom he lost. *My poor soul,* he sings,
my poor soul, I wouldn't trade you for anything.

Frederick the Pigeon & Why I'm a Student of the School of Misery

It's because I keep pulling the saddest detritus out of the world's hand
like this pigeon who doesn't know he should fly to Orlando, FL; the coffee

shop kids have named him Frederick; he squinches his head into his shoulder
looking like a millennial huddled beneath the outdoor table, rainbow tattoo

of feathers, iridescent, nonchalant. He's really an attractive bird but too young
for me. The band on his leg announces he already has an owner, anyway.

He's "registered," the coffee shop guy with smoothed-back fifties pomp, says.
He brings Frederick tiny cups of water, buys birdseed from "Wild Birds

Unlimited," and feeds him by hand while I take a walk backwards into my
own face. I type, "a prairie where deer approach out of the mist of my mind,"

while Frederick ambles clumsily through the propped open door. It's early dawn
inside my face now as I toss the Atlantic Ocean back and forth, the sound

of waves sucking pebbles behind my eyes. Frederick doesn't regret the islands
off the coast of New England where ferries fart their way over white caps,

and he doesn't know, will never know, who Marianne Moore is, but I've been
mulling over what she slighted as the "School of Misery": Robert, Sylvia, Anne,

John—because they couldn't keep their shit together on the page, their language
had stretch marks, line breaks, and heart breaks bursting from Boston. Why

Boston? I'm from Boston—is that why I imagine Frederick's emotions for him?
Is this emotional labor I'm performing for free? For a bird? So, his owner

picked up and moved from Tallahassee to Orlando, leaving him behind.
The coffee shop kids say they spoke to Frederick's bird abandoner over

the phone. He's not coming back to get Frederick. I wonder if Frederick's misery
qualifies him as a student of the "School of Misery"? The aging Marianne Moore

slept in the same bed with her mother. Two terse verses coiled back-to-back.
That sounds miserable to me. I prefer to think of a pigeon who is miserable,

really full of ennui, enough to fill an entire book of poetry. Or two. But that sounds like the inverse of misery—a pigeon embarking on a literary life.

My face keeps alternating attention between Frederick and the ocean I knew as a child. Out there on one of those islands Lowell exclaimed, "I myself am hell." Surely, he was miserable. Do you think a pigeon ever gets suicidal upon seeing squab on a menu? I can't even imagine feeling my mother's back pressed against mine in sleep, like Janus with two faces, poetry stitched into those spaces behind knees, the smalls of backs, necks curled like fiddleheads.

I'd fill those gaps with pigeons. All those feathers and coos like a living comforter—bumbling, clawing, gunmetal grey. Brilliant, but miserable.

In Praise of Being Lazy

Sway like the half-light of moon over
a football field so empty after midnight
you can hear the closest crickets making
love in the grass. Leave your shoes in piles
like they are snowflakes on Kilimanjaro &
you've developed a twenty-first century
allergy to footwear, like your toes protest
those coffins of leather and canvas, like you're
the infant learning to pull the socks off
her own feet to understand her first geography,
and why all the belts, laces, straps and strap
-ons when what we want is to loll beachside
beside the tide's lapping to stay in bed and taste
another minute undressed and unmade and let
the steam rise from our bodies, let the milk
curdle in the container. I'm done with guilt
that comes when I watch another, when I
binge, when I want to masturbate or sin
or stalk the exes on Facebook. I like to imagine
the world has no rules or fences or neighbors,
that not so long ago our parts were not separate,
that we were whole and holy and hot for life
that living was and still is the aphrodisiac
we miss when we confuse loneliness with being
alone, the praise-worthy sensation of wetting
your own lips, the pulse of a note struck
on a drum, the gurgle and hum of a baby
who knows all of this—how spring is a cell
within a cell within our blood a parade

on the red carpet, a sashay down
Broadway Boulevard, a coat with deep satin
pockets, a pair of tight jeans and a cut glass
necklace, an old photograph or a new bathing
suit, the smell of paper, a bookmark stuck
like a tongue between pages, a neon sign hung
in the heart and a hand on the cotton cord that
pulls it to turn us on and off and on and on again
until our Rockwell moment is lit for all eternity
in the buzz of some god's brain. Once, we thought
bees were dying and so we imagined what life
would be like after they were dead and gone
but then I saw the heads of the asters crooked
and janked with bees passing out in all their
glory and I remembered heaven is here
in the weeds, it is here, alive and breathing
sucking the yellow treat out of each day
and I am a particle on the back of yellow
and I am the bee and I am naked and hum
my god my god oh my god yes & please

Rockstar

I am lying in my bathtub when I hear it,
music coming from the HS playing field

loudspeakers. Over the chain link fence
the lacrosse players must have already

assembled. After two years of living next
door, I've grown used to hearing their

games—names and scores announced,
now Guns 'N Roses, a song I hate but

know by heart, how Axl Rose wants to
hide in her hair, how her eyes shouldn't

hold an ounce of pain and I think, now
as then, who is this chick with her empty

eyes, the target of so much desire she is
erased by it? In high school I wore a red

bandana on my head, danced by moving
my hips from side to side in a snake-like

motion while the boys watched from their
corners of the room. I let myself move

like that in the dark of the party because
I was being him, the Rockstar, his moves

were part of my costume that Halloween.
But, I wondered, how much must he or any

boy already have in their possession to want
a girl to hide inside of? No doubt they've

never felt it, how the world, at any moment,
could turn off its music, make her disappear.

Elegy for Two Former Lovers & One Ex-Husband

"And ghosts must do again
what gives them pain." —W. H. Auden

I.

He grows out his fingernails
so he can play sad songs on his guitar.

We park in my driveway kissing,
then I say, *Really, I have to go.* His body

is full of trap doors and passageways
and I'm not sure I want to know

where any of them lead.

II.

He tries to tell me
he loves me but stammers it

into my collarbone. When I ask him
to repeat what he's said, he replies,

Nothing. Never mind.

III.

I call it off during date number five
over dosas and mattar paneer,

his mango lassi and my Sprite. He balls

the paper straw wrapper
passes it between fingertips. Maybe

I'm more into his collections of masks
and art deco furniture than him.

I have a habit of being collected.

IV.

We can hold everything in abeyance, lie
on the bed staring up between the slats

of the plastic blinds. The parking lot lamps
shine pickets of light across our torsos.

We hear a disembodied voice
announcing the score from a nearby stadium.

Touchdown! It says.

V.

Desire asks me to make a shape
out of something shapeless. How many times

will I get it wrong? Half of a bedroom set,
two bookshelves, desk, futon, big screen T.V.

and his grandmother's lazy boy chair,
the wreckage of his marriage.

Adorable, I say.

VI.

I go to work and feel I'm in a dream,
return to him and feel I'm in reality.

The universe, we're making it. We touch
the edge of space like we're silkworms

spinning light between our bodies,
both of us repeating, *I want, I want,*

and the other saying *Yes, me too. I want too.*

VII.

When I point to a bottle
of hydrocodone that my ex-husband

has left behind, he swallows some
when he thinks I'm not watching.

We grill steaks and eat Oreo cookies.
Later, he pukes in the master bathroom.

I throw out the rest of the pills
while he sleeps, then climb in, hold him.

VIII.

For ten years I'm wife
to a naval officer. I tell the story

of my marriage like this: Our first
year—he prefers to puzzle new

brick into the patio. Each time I look out
the window or step outside he's there,

in the yard, sentinel of hours. Most nights
I set his dinner in the fridge.

IX.

Here, I think, is a cove full of honey,
the kind of vine that's full of white sails

angling backwards in the wind.
They lift their nothing. For each lover

I called out, was razor thin—a quiet
lashing me to him, and him, and him.

Anti-Ode to Tallahassee, Florida

Sure, there were one or two picturesque harbors if you
squinted your eyes as you drove by long after midnight

so the lapping waves seemed to make an overture of love
to the docks, the sailboats cheek to cheek nestled flush,

their fiberglass hulls scarping the buoys into a gold-specked
salt brine where moonlight sluiced its juice. The herons

and pelicans forever strutting those Florida shores mouthing
off to manatees and those cousins of the dinosaurs, alligators

with feathers between their teeth. Ungodly country where I'd
jog along sandy paths launching myself from mile three

to dancing the cancan over another slithering stick awoken
by some primordial hand of God which still works

its alpha and omega on every snake between the Okefenokee
Swamp and Devil's Sink. The whole landscape grouchy

with spiked palms, and spiders the size of palms, a blast-zone
of leftover divine creativity like a painter's palette of knockout

colors except for the tedium of beiges and browns, and army
greens, pine pollen yellows, turquoise baby blues, and oysters

on the half-shell, rancid pilings, and aren't pelicans just the ugliest
birds you've ever seen? Not a sauce in all creation that could

make that bird look edible. Whenever I tried to stroll, or drive
to the beach, every inch of me would spritz so I'd wish again

for the nucleus of home, the A/C. Even the rain wouldn't be
outdone, storms on LSD, storm sandwiches, clouds as big

as Zeus's butt cheeks, lightning bugs and their neon-love
abdomens, my car turned gold over night from pine pollen

glazed with thick droplets of sap I'd remove with rubbing
alcohol. The earth so sandy it seemed a personal favor it didn't

inter our whole town—gone Bird's Aphrodisiac Oyster Shack,
gone Poor Paul's Pourhouse, gone Fire Betty's Arcade and Railroad

Square where I'd spent many a First Friday walking the small
circle of your esplanade of dander-and-mildew-crowded

vintage shops, and how many food carts? Seven? And one
anemic drum circle in the corner of that haven, a pod

of junior hippies at their spinach and bongos. So what if I
headed west, can you blame me when my morning ritual

was coffee, eyedrops, and several antihistamines? And now
that I live a coast apart I suck and savor at the bones

of Tallahassee, that gobstopper of grief and overfed
in-bred geese that haunted Ella Lake, the thick, heady scent

of jasmine, honeysuckle, the inner-tube of humid air,
the cicadas back in their offices pulling another all-nighter,

the open windows full of yesterday's spiders' webs, someone
up the road playing fiddle on their porch, and whoever kept

practicing in the high school batting cages—clink and clink
they aimed into the dark which answered back. Clink, clink.

The Drive-thru at Rosa's

The land where your house is built was once gold,
desperate as a coin placed in a reservation slot machine.
When your father drives through town in his Corolla
he feels small again, like he could park all day, listen
to the dusty wind cut the feed lots and be forgotten.
Already we've ridden to the drive-thru at Rosa's three
times to sate our craving for beef tacos. I say there must
be drugs in their tortillas. Here everyone's got something
bigger than you; hair, trucks, stomachs. It's an hour
to the New Mexico border where the red sand makes
ancient patterns if seen from above. At night I make you
walk with me around the subdivision. We step on fallen
acorns from the trees. Someone's mother is making Chex
mix in her kitchen; they watch Fox News while I think
coyotes are drinking water from cattle troughs, their noses
wet with blood, their ears are still twitching. This place
is sun-drenched, no more than desert. Water knows
to retreat to unexplored depths. The cotton farmers give
their children less and less. What was once plentiful now
hides behind fences where I know there are guns and people
who believe in them. Yesterday, near the Coke machine,
I saw a little girl, long dark hair in a braid as thick as
my wrist. *Mama, Mama,* she said to the woman
sweeping the floor beneath the tables.

Self Portrait as Daughter Stuffed with a Sack of Pomegranates

One busted pipe beneath the sink where water
    and day-old carrot juice leaked and the rind
of the avocado, misshapen testicle, the brown
    seed like a promise that all hardness comes
to bear fruit, the dial of the cat's paws mapping
    the stained concrete, a wet symphony of notes

imprecise and fleeting as I touch my face
    in the mirror with concealer after sopping up
what I knew were the traces of last night's
    dream, my father by a dry riverbed, shadows
between mesquite trees, black-blood-sap,
    trunks the width of a girl's thigh, wind

toppling backwards into seams where water
    should cover stones, the dust of our deceased,
the mirror explaining to me the uses of a life,
    or light, or mascara, of dabbing saffron red
in the center and placing my father where I
    can see him as I drive to work, my car's hood

pitted from semis on the highways that throw
    grit and gravel, the windshield with star-
burst I haven't yet bothered to get fixed, can't
    bring myself to think too long on the miles
I've driven to Texas, Colorado, stops in
    Arkansas and Tennessee where I slept

in a cabin on the edge of a dirt road, little fire
    in the stove, power lines arching the sky
but inside I kept oil in the lamp, fire burning
    down, the thrushes in the twiggy branches
scattered their divinity like popcorn kernels
    popped in air I can't eat, or taste the things

I've refused, the liverwurst my boss spread on
    whole wheat, the giving up of coffee, sugar,
meat; the times I vomited myself into believing
    I could heal this way, by emptying myself
of me. The husband I stumbled behind until
    I spoke only in the softest syllables I could

find, the hush and dish of a wanna-be-mother
    to a newborn trying to keep him calm. Once
I leapt like fire into a man and burned like a god
    asking what could come after me? Who
could come after? I became a one-woman
    -apocalypse my bare-back ride into turquoise

calling it orange, calling it December, calling it
    wheat bending gold beneath your palm, sun-
warmed and lit with tiny heads of flame, you
    learn to hold your father in you like you are
a cradle, like every busted pipe in your life is
    the opposite of trouble, it is not metaphorical

or singing to you about rivers or the lake you walk
    to on the edge of what seems, what has always
seemed, an almost memory, a snake-in-the-grass
    kind of lake, the hair-standing-up-on-the-back
-of-your-neck kind of daughter, the thirsty kind
    of daughter with a sack of pomegranates instead

of a womb. She leaves seeds everywhere she goes,
     a constellation of juice, a geography of mouths
she fills. She is in labor, like paradise opening
     between her legs, animals on the deck of her body,
an ark strung in a tree that bends like a moon scar
     growing from the hole in her father's head.

Last December

I opened my life along its spine, a new blue emerged,
two halves jolted apart like lips once frozen around
an ocean. Words can roll like peas from one side
of a plate to another like waves through a brain.
The skull begins soft, spoon-sized fontanelle, a new
blue in the brain. I once saw a human brain cut in two,
soft as pudding, grey as winter sea foam bursting
as though from the long throats of cranes. Tonight
I've set my table—new plates, blue folded cloth
napkins to fly between my friends' laps and their faces
cut in two, we fold into one another as if undressing
in the shadows of a sycamore tree, the plates of our faces
erased. We stack each on each our sable irises, our darkness,
evening pressing us as gentle as God's voice slipping upon
the cosmos. I strum along. He floats between me and what I
mean to be. On my knees, light goes everywhere I go. It's
how I know to praise the sycamore trees, a new blue,
the ring of light that goes where I go, arrives slow as bone.

The Lying Field

I climbed out windows at night to be alone,
believed that the house where I'd slept for years

had thickened into a wood, that the carpets
were riddled with hyacinth bulbs sucked deep

into a synthetic winter. Memories I held still like cups
of spring I did not want to spill. It was all storytelling,

who we'd become, our names with their mystery
of syllables, the self cradled in curves of tongue

and lilt of dialect. How many times had my thumb
pressed a door latch so I could escape? So I'll admit

I've stumbled into each new translation of self,
have woken at dawn to listen to the neighbor's dog

barking at November, again, unnoticed. Tell me what
other distance is there that we've stashed between us?

We lie in or to the fields and still they believe.

She Wonders if She is Still in Love

There's a beauty I no longer want
    to talk about, it settles in the dry season,
        the air full of red dirt stirring like wonder

        around the swing set in the yard. It's why
    I've kept so many feathers, the yellow-tipped
cedar waxwing, the ruby throat

of the hummingbird, which we both
    know can fly backwards I liken to your
        passion. And as if I see you in all things

        you uncloak in me a blessing of leaves
    strewn to the floor, untangle the limbs of trees
from my wrists. I can say I've been patient

but that would be a lie. I pretend I am waiting,
    but in my mind we've been together a thousand
        years. I am the wind learning how to be the sun;

        I am already defeated in my wanting. So I try
    to taste you as I settle for everyone but you.
I watch for your moods to fly by

in equations of birds. I go outside alone
    strung and fluttering with moths, wait
        for night to come and unbuckle my mouth.

When I Saw You at the Party Friday Night

It was as if I'd been kneeling. You were like a fat lime weighing
down its branch. In the dark, the moment began searching for its

own applause in my pulse. Because you were there (but not mine)
I wanted to fill my bed with everyone's laughter and everyone

you spoke to or laid eyes on; your words and gestures held
like smoke in evening's glass. The seedlings in the garden began

shivering with night's breezes, the humidity settled on everyone's
skin. Just then the cicadas entered their valley of complaint

and I was hollowed of the place where you'd once been—fields,
fences, decay, but what do I know of such things, or even

what is real? *More*, the body says, *more*, and my heart drags
its tired head up and glances from a far edge as if it's been

puzzling out a way to return to you. When everyone standing near
me is already loved & still so lonely, all our wants look the same.

I was trying to memorize the shape of what had once felt endless,
and I was kneeling, and you were the lime waiting on its branch.

Her Notes on Texas Wind

I watch what must be a beech tree outside the window
of my Airbnb, a shattering of green and one thin pane;
I've used so many borrowed utensils today
fork, spoon, a dull ceramic knife to cut
avocado and onion, an over-cooked sweet potato

in a convection oven. I am only miles away
from where I once climbed up on the roof of our old house
storm system visible across the miles
flat roads that looked as if they could end at ocean
but there was only more desert, more dust, the tar shingles

knocking above us until I laid that ladder to the rain gutter
and climbed up with a hammer in my hand as if I could
knock on the ceiling of sky, against God's eye
and find myself without him, without a husband,
alone at last wrapped in blue. I carried three nails

between my lips, tense, and with purpose
always a nail begging to be put still into a coffin
of wood, to make its slow spark of metal rent together
the pieces of lives, as marriage does, the very word
a screw and a drill. Do you think it strange that it was I

who rose above our home that night, crawled across
to loosening shingles and one by one took the wet nails
from my mouth? I must admit it was a rush, all that wind,
and I believed I could see straight to Lubbock, Texas,
or was it Amarillo, yellow star or rose of the panhandle?

Strange how when I turned my face up I forgot about
the distance, so captivated by open sky like an afterthought,
like every wife spent evenings on rooftops hammered
by wind, nailing her life down thinking to let it fly away
into some new pasture so raw and green it's almost blue.

She Addresses Her Unborn Children

Night like the arc of a swan's
   neck or blown like salt across a table
      but inside we are fruit, the upside-down

violet prairie of a fig in a child's
   mouth, his collection of stars. I have
      no son or daughter but if I did I'd teach

them to be soft the way fog might
   capture the question of their bodies,
      tentative, languid in a release of dawn,

the scent of apples, the scent of rain
   that made us. Beneath the chill frost
      we are still damp, earth-clung, full

of memories, seedlings that germinate
   in spite of night's excesses of hunger
      and love. I will always be tender

at your feet and lips, cup your spine
   to curve where you curve. The way
      moss and shadows pull the breath

from us, you'll carry your hands open,
   palm the soil on either side. We are
      ancient, simple vocabularies

tasting what hangs from the hooks
in our flesh, the flesh of the flesh
that made us.

When I Come Back from the Dead

There are no doorbells. The tulips greet me
with the same empty cups I've never been

able to drink from. The porch lights,

left on all night, have battened their faces
against the confusion of moths.

There was a time when any hand—your hand

was the entire world at work on its old
dissertation about love. That word locked

in page after page of thinking. The ambulance

inside me has only just turned
off its siren. I've learned to hover, to fly

backwards into the ravaged heads

of cardinals. The way love works is
darkness, darkness, darkness, let there be

one atomic and particular sun—a body
will speak fire into itself, an opal ring

lit. The world will then reverse its grip.

References

The poem "Pistol of Bones" is titled after "El genio de la especie: huesos formando una pistola" by Wolfgang Paalen.

The poem "Rockstar" refers to the Guns & Roses song "Sweet Child 'O Mine."

The poem "Self Portrait as a Delicate Fly" is titled after Lenora Carrington's sculpture "Fina mosca."

Lines from "In the City of Light," by Larry Levis, are quoted in the poem, "Poem with a Mouse & a Line by Larry Levis."

Acknowledgments

Many thanks to the editors of the following journals, anthologies, and websites where these poems originally appeared:

Adroit Journal: "Eleven"; *Best New Poets 2017*: "Last December" selected by Natalie Diaz; *Best New Poets 2019*: "Poem with a Mouse & a Line by Larry Levis" published as "Poem in a Duplex with Mouse & a Line by Larry Levis" selected by Cate Marvin; *blackbird*: "Blue Eyed Crow" published as "Weightless"; *Blue Earth Review*: "Disassembling the Navy Wife" published as "Relics"; *Connotation Press*: "Lying on a Bench in Dorothy B Oven Park I'm Mistaken for a Homeless Woman" and "The Navy Wife's Plan for Her Wedding Dress"; *Crazyhorse*: "The Ant & the Our Father"; *Fourteen Hills*: "Go to the Edge of Giving then Break Yourself"; *Meridian Magazine*: "It's Not an Apocalypse if the Horses are Mortal" winner of the 2018 Meridian Editors Prize, "The Navy Wife Talks in Her Sleep" runner-up for the 2017 Meridian Editors Prize; *Mid-American Review*: "The Lying Field"; *Minnesota Review*: "Slow Parting"; *Mississippi Review*: "The Goddess of Confusion" published as "The World's Trespass on the Body's Central Disruption" finalist for their 2016 Poetry Prize; *Moon City Review*: "When I Come Back from the Dead"; *Narrative Magazine*: "Peaches" and "Frederick the Pigeon & Why I'm a Student of the School of Misery"; *New Ohio Review*: "Like a Fish Needs a Bicycle"; *New South Journal*: "She Addresses her Unborn Children" published as "Lessons in the Provenance of Living" third place winner of their 2016 Poetry Contest; *Nimrod Journal*: "When the Mississippi Speaks with its Wet, Pretty Mouth" "Assembling the Navy Wife" published as "The Navy Wife Tries on Her Body"

"Pistol of Bones" and "She & Wolf" which were selected as a finalist for the 2019 Pablo Neruda Prize for Poetry; *Prairie Schooner:* "The Difference Between a Raven & a Crow" and "Her Notes on Texas Wind"; *Puerto del Sol:* "Unfuckable Poem"; *Quarter After Eight:* "Elegy for Two Former Lovers & One Ex-Husband"; *Rattle:* "After Joining OkCupid" published as "After Joining OkCupid, Desire Becomes a Periscope on Distance"; *Salamander:* "The Drive-thru at Rosa's" published as "The Land Where Your House is Built"; *South Dakota Review:* "When I Saw You at the Party Friday Night"; *Stirring Lit:* "Poem with a Mouse & a Line by Larry Levis" published as "Poem in a Duplex with Mouse & a Line by Larry Levis"; *Zone 3:* "Waveland Mississippi, an Elegy" and "Naked in Cowboy Boots with Lasso I Challenge God."

Thank you to the editors of *Verse Daily* for featuring "Waveland Mississippi, an Elegy." Thank you to *Passages North* for choosing "Blue Eyed Crow" listed as "Weightless" as a finalist for the 2017 Elinor Benedict Poetry Prize, and "Rockstar" as a finalist for the 2019 Elinor Benedict Poetry Prize. Thank you to the editors of *Palette Poetry* for selecting "Self Portrait as Daughter Stuffed with a Sack of Pomegranates" as a finalist for the 2019 Palette Poetry Prize, additional thanks to *Gulf Coast* and Chen Chen for selecting this poem as a 2018 Gulf Coast Prize honorable mention. Thank you to the editors of *Bettering American Poetry* for selecting "Eleven" for their 2019 anthology.

I am grateful to the many teachers and mentors I've had the good fortune to study with over the past several years as well as my thesis committees at University of North Texas and UNC Greensboro, and my dissertation committee at Florida State University including: Rebecca Black, Bruce Bond, Henri Cole, Bryan Cuevas, Stuart Dischell, Barbara Hamby, Terry Kennedy, David Kirby, Corey Marks, Diane Roberts, David Roderick, Patricia Smith, and Robert Stilling. Without